A Splendiferous Multifarious Life

Achint Malhotra

BookLeaf Publishing

India | USA | UK

Presentation by *BookLeaf Publishing*

Web: www.bookleafpub.com

E-mail: info@bookleafpub.com

ISBN: 9789358319569

First edition 2023

PREFACE

This book actually emerges from a sea of poems that I have been compiling since I was 13.

A Longing For A Friend

I've had so many laughs with you
We talked for hours
We went crazy wild under the city lights
But I woke up, it was all a dream.

We're best friends......
In my imagination, we're best friends
My head in your lap,
Yours in mine,
Laughing for hours,
Joking the whole time.

Riding a rollercoaster of joy,
with its twisty turns, we travel through life with
no goodbyes.

Pulling pranks,
Mischievous plans,
In my imagination, we have the best time of our
lives.

Only in my imagination.

Daddy

As I lie in a pool of pain,
I'm always trying not to drown.

I kick my legs, I kick them hard
But pain is an ocean I have to swim across:
My daughter & son are waiting for me
On an island that's so close, yet so far from me.

I can make it, I have made it this far
I have to.....

Pain is a mountain I have to climb
My hands hurt, my feet hurt, I might drop & die.
But my daughter & son are waiting for me, on
the top that is so close, yet so far from me.

I can make it, I have made it this far
I have to....

Time's a ticking and my daughter's a killing
My son is silently dying
Can I make it? Can I make it this far?

I have to.

So I'll swim hard, I'll cry hard, I'll climb every
mountain.
I will make it, I will make it this far.
That is true.

Alone at Loss

Loss. It hits you like a truck, doesn't it?

Losing your loved one.
Losing your credit card.
Losing your keys.
LOSING YOUR MIND.

Losing anything of dear value.........
Just plain sucks doesn't it?

Lovely was the spirit that I lost. What a lovely
person he was.
Child was the spirit in my heart that went along
with him.
I mourned the death of not one but two souls
that night.

What is loss anyway? Huh?
What is loss?
The dictionary definition of loss is: "the state or
feeling of grief when deprived of someone or
something of value."

Quite frankly, I'm at a loss for words right now.
Things like loss & heartbreak are supposed to
get me to write but.....I'm just in loss.

I'm stranded alone on the island, I'm alone on the
top of the mountain.
My brain is empty
My heart is hollow
I'm scraping the edges of my skull to gather bits
of my brain but can't find much.
I'm scraping my heart for a feeling yet, I'm at a
loss.

A Longing for a Friend II

I was driving on twisty roads under the sunny
sun, having long conversations with you.
...........They were all imaginary (and you weren't
there at all)

I was in the bathroom arguing over our silent
friendship
With you who was not there.
............Just me alone in the mirror.

What are you doing, now?
Where are you?

Are we ever gonna meet again? I wonder now.
How?
I don't wanna die with these imaginations
unlived.

They're bursting through me right now.
I really wish we could meet right now.
I really want a best friend right now.

Don't Leave. Please Stay.

I grew up in a fantasy fortress made of dreams
And I decorated it with my sweetest memories.
But as the fortress grew bigger, the memories
got bitter.
But, then I found you lurking
You didn't realise you were there, but you were
there.
And you're still here. You never left.
And I don't want you to leave my fantasy
fortress made up of dreams.

That's the world I created, and that's where you'll
stay:
In my fantasy fortress made up of dreams
And I'll never let you leave.
I'll captivate you with glitter and things.
My magical world of enchanting things.

Just you & me playing in the garden
Riding the carpet
Swimming the ocean
High on love potion

We'll decorate our Christmas tree with our sweet
memories.

Joy, love and laughter in our fortress of dreams.

8

Beautiful Brain

I must admit it was the intelligence
The intelligence got to me

You can work wonders and create magic with
that brain.
Thousands of wires, intertwining with each
other, firing up that knowledge & bizarre
creativity.

Yes! That creativity!
When my eyebrows raised at the unexpected
genius of yours.
While we were choosing from the options, you
created your own road that was sweet, simple
and genius.

Oh, what a beautiful brain of yours!
You produce solutions for others
Oh, what beauty!
I wonder what it's like in that quiet brain of
yours:
Does it bloom with colour? Design pattern? Or
is it Golden Silent?

Oh, but when your brain chooses to annoy,
chooses to destroy, is it still beautiful?
Is beauty only good?
Do you still have a beautiful brain even when
you choose to annoy and destroy?

Yes, there's a beauty in that
Because there's a heart in that
Because there's a human in that
Otherwise, we're delusional robots

Your brain is beautiful. Even when it spits fire,
it's beautiful.
But the brain is perhaps at its peak beauty when
it produces a heart.
A feeling, a tear, a smile, a little fear, a cackle of
laughter or just plain despair.

Our brain works in numerous ways but the best
most beautiful is when it shows care.

The First Traces of Envy

You are my best friend
How could you so?
You are His best friend
How could you so?
You haunt my nights
And contaminate my brain
with infectious envy and hate

But you are my best friend
Oh God, how could you so?
Teach me your ways
So that I might befriend him
Just like you did

Sometimes I want to be you........even when I
know it's best not to
But most importantly I need to be with him
And I'm ready to climb over you.

Midnight Thought

I love, I love and love
I much, much much
I heart less and brain more
Am I heartless or am I cold?

Am I loveless or a child?
In Wonderland or just deprived?
I Hatter more and I quiet more
I weird more and I calculate more
Am I a child or am I cold?
In Wonderland or surrounded by less more?

Do I have love? Do I have muchness? Or am I
just a robot roasting my daily lunch of loveness?
Am I a brain who just eats my heart?
Or am I a heart, sanctuarised in my brain?

Either way, I know:
I heart less and brain more
I'm a child with a bit of cold
A body surrounded by less more and a soul in
richness of the Wonderland world.
I have loveness in my soul and a robot for my
form
I love and love and love

I much and much and much
I know and know such

13

Mr. Flattery Words

So orderly, eloquent and deliberate are your
words
You communicated every emotion perfectly
Except, the human soul

The human soul is messy, and intense
It is a complex array of emotions and sometimes
they don't make any sense
Yet, you've written about this using big big
words and fully organized stanzas.

How could you?
Either you're a genius
Or just fancy
A poet
Or just a wannabe
A writer
Or someone who wants to sound like one
How could you?
How could you betray me such?

I went to you to find the words to describe the
high tides and storms
that rage inside my soul

The bitter bits of good and evil that wriggle my
brain into playing tricks
I want to understand it all, I want to describe it
all

But you!
With your fancy moustache and your fancy pen
Your fancy diary and your pretentious verse
You can't translate the human soul!
You can't translate the wants, the needs, the
desires, the temptations, the love, the sin that
lives inside our soul!
You can't translate my soul!

Who are you? And what do you write? Where is
it coming from?

I WANT TO WRITE

I swim in the sea of words that are in my
notebook
And as I take a deep dive, I try to find letters to
cling to, words that'll reach the surface
Words that'll one day describe what I truly want
to
However, I want to
And people will like it.

But sometimes as I dive,
I can't cling to any letters,
I start to drown
Nothing reaches the surface
My notebook is empty and I can't breathe

I shake in desperation,
I choke in the panic discretion,
"I can't write anything!", I say
"I can't find anything!", I say

Am I a writer?
Am I a poet?
Am I a vulture?
My brain is wringing its juice, desperate to
produce.

Produce something that can touch the heart of
someone
Produce something that can kill the heart of
someone
Produce something that can restore the heart of
someone

I wanna create something that the world won't
forget,
I wanna create something that the world hasn't
seen, yet.
I have the voice, I have the pen, I have the brain,
so let's get this going then.

My Crown

My castle, my throne, my crown
But the curse of being a child, I frown.

The King is dead; his castle, my castle; his
throne, my throne; his crown, my crown
But "They"!
They get to make the decisions around
And I am buried in shackles to the ground

This curse of being a princess, I'm through
I'm the Queen, I Am, I make the Rule.

So come at me with your duels
I'll fight each and every single one of you

It's my castle, my throne, my crown!
So why am I the one who's paraded around?
Why am I the child who always understands?
I wanna break free and rule again!

"Never kill the child in you", but I've had
enough!
This child is always never grown up
I'll Kill it, this Child in Me
I wear my crown, but they say it's too big for me

I sit on my throne, but they, "When you grow up"
It's my castle but, "you can't make any noise"

I'm done! I'm through! With this child in me!
I'm done! Now I wanna rule the seas!
I'm through with this child in me!

Little Child

When I see the little child
I see me
I miss her dearly
Daddy kissed her goodnight,
told her a bedtime story: one day, he is gonna
return and wake her up dearly

She's still asleep, the little dearie
That little girl, I miss me
I see her fast asleep, buried peacefully under my
responsibilities

Oh wake up dearie, please,
don't leave me
It was just a bedtime story,
He's never coming, is he?

"I have friends"

Remember when we were running towards the
future and my dress got stuck in the tree branch?
I let you keep going and no one looked back.

I stood up alone and caught up
"I made it", I say
"We didn't notice you were behind", they say
"But we've already made many plans", they say,
"Care to join?"

I don't wanna go: self-respect
I don't wanna be lonely: I introspect
I know they don't wait for me, and sometimes
may not notice me, but they were nice enough to
smile at me.

I think I'm just gonna let the wolves eat me.
I don't wanna be lonely: I introspect
"You dumbo! " yells my self-respect

"I love them anyway", I confess, "It is nice to
have people around"

Maybe they love me too.

A Longing

Take me to a place beyond comprehension
Take me to a place beyond understanding
A place where all the nonsense makes sense
Where the fun is a never-end

O' take me to a place that doesn't exist
I wanna see a world that I can't describe
And I wanna see it with new eyes
And I wanna come back with a new state of
mind.

Beyond imagination, time and space, I want to
go to a place that doesn't exist.

The Visionary

I am a wandering creature, yet lost
I am a curious creature, yet satisfied
Satisfied with the already discovered nature but
with the urge to discover more.

My toes dancing, flowing with the grass.
My hands touching the lost sun
My spine laid on the rocky surface of the moon

Ready to touch the sky, ready to face the doom
Ready to fly to the stars,
Ready to fall on face, hard

I am a woman looking for adventures, living
with scars, looking for more laughs; looking for
life,
And I know where to start.

F*ck Hardwork!

Don't you ever get fed up?
That beautifully chaotic relationship, don't you
ever wanna end it?
That last push to make it, why take it?
The ladder to the top, why climb it?
I'm so sick of it!
"Where there's a will, there's a way", they say
"Work hard", they say
I'm downright beginning to hate it!

"Why?", I ask, "what for?"
Don't get me wrong, I believe everyone has to
work hard
But that doesn't mean that I like it
Staying up all night for a grade that won't matter
in the future?
Why is it worth it?
A disguised memory test determining my
future? Our future?
What kind of a joke is this?

I work hard, but I just gotta say this once, it is
how we perhaps feel at some point in our lives:
f*ck hard work!

Feelings I can't control, Feelings that won't go; The Sparkling Tangerine

Once upon a time,
I visited a land full of friends and happiness
And ended up contracting a disease

The early symptoms were light,
my eyes couldn't budge and I was curious as to
why

Then I heard a doctor say,
"Flutterings are never good news"
And then I knew, there was something wrong
with me

Once upon a time,
I revisited that land to find out why I was at such
dis-ease
What could it be, that was bothering me?

It was the Sparkling Tangerine that I ate at the
fair,
And now it is inside of me, sparkling
And I'm just waiting for it to go away, kindly.

Once upon a time,
The tangerine came alive and it started to eat
me, from the inside.
I panicked, when will it go away? When will it
stop?
I visited the loo every day, but no luck, it was
here to stay.

The doctor said he couldn't help me
I went back to the fair,
The Tangerine stand had disappeared and a
storm began to rage; I realised I'd never be the
same. And part of me had changed.

Stupid Tangerine, sparkling inside of me, please
leave, kindly

Will The Real God Please Stand Up?

I'm praying,
who is listening?
Hello? Is anyone there?

I'm just a little human who doesn't know beyond
earth
I don't know who you are, or where you are, but
can you hear me?
People tell me, "Ours is real", but then others tell
me, "No this one is", but which one is, at least
can you hear me, right?

So you, the real One, could you please stand up?
Mortals on earth who have never seen you are
trying to tell me about you and their stories
confuse me
In fact, a lot of them are contradictory!

So will the real God please stand up?
Because they tell me to come to you at my
worst, but I can't even find you at my best
There are so many of you and yet, there is only
one, so tell me who are you?

I'm praying,
are you listening? Is there anyone to answer the
door I'm knocking?
I'm waiting.....

My Lament

The lovely clouds that fly, that shape the entire
sky,
pass us by but go unnoticed
The lovely green grass that comes alive at times,
that fills the garden with a sort of laughter and
shine, goes unnoticed.

Various absurd times, disguised as green, call us
to explore His creation.

The lovely blue seas that shine like floating
crystals,
the lovely sand that sparks like crystals and the
lovely black sky that is filled with ethereal
crystals, but it goes unnoticed.

People sit there in a closed-off shelter called a
shop, looking for a crystal to show off.
Yet they forget about the natural crystals of our
world that are already there,
waiting to be looked upon,
waiting for its complexities to be explored.

I lament, my heart laments, my brain laments.

I feel sorry for those who don't sit down and take
a break.
I grieve for those who don't sit down and let
their thoughts astray because in the end,
It just tells me that they're slaves.

Slaves to the work that has kept their brains in a
cage,
a stranger to the tiniest to tallest well-decorated
complexities that surround us.

A stranger to its wild and crazy natural home,
come on man, even the wild creatures of our
home are a beauty, provoke curiosity that you
seem not to have.

So, let your brain run away and run wild
Let your brain have its rest and you have yours

Escape to the wonders of the hidden worlds in
our big world

And one day I hope I won't have to lament about
the slaves, the caged feeble brains.

Wonder

I wonder when it is July,
I wonder why the sky is so high,
I wonder everything about my life.

I wonder if the stove is left on
I wonder if my homework is all done
I wonder where my brother's arun
I wonder if I can make a Poly Pie
I wonder if that Perriwocky on my wall turns
tides
I wonder if I can ever make it to the skies

Oh! I wonder, I wonder, I wonder and I wonder,
the list never dies.
I could fill up outer space with my list but then
space will run out of space to fit my
never-ending list.

The core of the Big Apple in USA, I wonder if
I'll ever go there to stay
The nuclear fusion, I see every day in the day,
truly a wonder, delight!
The core of the Big Apple in USA, why is it an
apple anyway?

June, July, May, August,
How does the human form from dust?
April, May, June, July,
Did I mess up the order in that first line? *sigh*

Oh! I wonder, I wonder, I wonder and I wonder,
the reality of our lives.
Are we born to die?
Why are we given such lives?
Why are these pests feasting upon the innocence
of the future lives?

The innocents on the streets turned from green
to dark,
Earth is always half in the dark, I cannot help
but wonder about those innocents living in the
dark.

I question the lives of people on the ground.
Why are they feasted upon by the dead hound?
Why were they born of this fate, O' Serpent you
are to be blamed.

The Serpent, I wonder,
What would be of our lives
If that you hadn't destroyed His perfect plans?

Depression, anxiety, hate, corruption, angry,
fighting, war, bloodshed,

It took a snake to form this definition of real life,
If we were in the Garden Of Eden,
You'd have probably had a life.

This is the beauty of Wonder,
The fuel to seek more about life,
The befores and afters, the ifs and whys and the
wonders,
It is the way we find the wild, the crazy, the
unbelievable, the unfathomable, the miracle,
It is the way that we find Life.

Praise

Praise, praise, but what, the bloody craze?
The craze of what, the ultimate chase,
Of life being treated like a bloody race?

Nah, if I'm gonna praise, I'll praise the worn-out
faces,
Helping to save this race,
I'll praise the captains, the soldiers, the doctors,
the mohawks.
I'll praise the God, the Heavens, the Devil, the
angels and whatnot.

What is praise truly?
The chase of the bloody craze,
Of a person who attracted a bloody race?

If only I knew what praise truly was, I could
give everyone that temporary crown.
Praise, praise, it is a good idea to be sure but
what's with bloody craze?

Why not praise the homeless guy,
who leaps from the streets, into the sky, does big
things, even if it is only in his dreams?

Why not praise the devil, who has so far
somehow managed to stay, still?
There is no craze but don't they deserve some
bloody craze?

Oh, what O' what is praise?
Let me tell you, it is just to tell, to the person
who once fell, that you did a good job, even
though he is in hell.
It is saying "Oh well done my lad!" with a big
smile of glad,
To the homeless chap to Gods of the skies,
To the birds that fly to creatures in the ground
nearby.

"You've made it this far, congratulations my
friend!
you've managed to be hated all the 745 years of
your life!"
Tis' was not sarcastic, just to make sure,
"You've swum the seas, and battled the
dolphins, you've climbed the Everest and hunted
Goblins, you did a good job and I thank ye man
for the power of your endorphins"

Good or bad, with craze or without, everyone
deserves a little praise for sure,
A little something good, that be the ear's food,
A tiny saying, sweeping the face shiny,

With a tiny smile sparkling.
After all, a praise is just sunlight,
warming the little man stuck in an igloo at the
cold heights.

"I'm the sunlight", it says, "I'll give you a little
helping hand, I will take you out of the cold and
bring in the bright, I will give you a little jetpack
ride!
I know who's bad, I know who's good, I know
the cold seas that you've swum through, I know
the Goblins that almost killed you.

I'll hold your hand and give you strength, I'll fix
your spine, I'll pull your head high,
I'll give you wine and bring you back from the
dead,

But don't you fright, from your lone journey
ahead,
It's okay, cause just a little praise goes a long
way".